POSITIVELY PREHISTORIC JOKES

Compiled by Alex Demetris

TOP THAT! Kids™

Copyright © 2004 Top That! Publishing plc,
Tide Mill Way, Woodbridge, Suffolk, IP12 1AP, UK
Top That! is a Registered Trademark of Top That! Publishing plc.
All rights reserved.
www.topthatpublishing.com

Why do triceratops' only have three horns?

Because they're too stupid to count to four!

Why was the albino mammoth so useless?

He was a white elephant!

What do you call a dinosaur with glasses?

Do-you-fink-he-saurus!

Why was the caveman late for work?

Because the wheel hadn't yet been invented!

What do you call the
dinosaur police?

Tricera-cops!

Why did
the velociraptor cross the road?
Because she hadn't evolved into a
chicken yet!

What's Nelly the elephant's
granny called?

Nelly the woolly mammoth!

Why couldn't the diplodocus ever
make his mind up?

He was afraid to stick his neck out!

Where do mammoths go shopping?

Woolworths!

What is the motto of heavy metal dinosaurs?

Tyrannosaurus ROCKS!

What is Neanderthal Man's favourite starter?

Primordial soup!

Where do female dinosaurs go to buy their clothes?

Triceratop-shop!

What do you get when you cross a dinosaur with a wizard?

A tyrannosaurus hex!

What do you a call dinosaur with one eye?

I dino.

Who is the most popular dinosaur psychic?

Mystic Steg(osaurus)!

Why did the archaeologist get locked out of the museum?

He had forgotten his skeleton key!

Who is the funkiest dinosaur?

Disco-saurus!

What do dinosaurs use to power their cars?

Fossil fuel!

Knock knock!
Who's there?
Terry.
Terry who?
Terry-Dactyl!

Knock knock!
Who's there?
Tracey.
Tracy who?
Tracy-Ratops!

Who is the best writer in the prehistoric world?

Charlotte Brontë-saurus!

What game do diplodocus' play with cavemen?

Squash!

Why did the mammoth put his trunk across the path?

To trip up the cavemen!

Why wouldn't the T-Rex pay to use a 'speak your weight' machine?

He had his own scales!

What kind of tiles won't stick on your wall?

Rep-tiles!

What did the polite T-Rex say to the caveman?

Pleased to eat you!

Why did the dinosaur breeder call his brontosaurus 'Fog'?

Because he was grey and thick!

How could the cavewoman tell the velociraptor had been in her fridge?

There were claw prints in the trifle!

What is big and scaly and bounces up and down?

An iguanadon on a pogo stick!

What do you get if you cross an allosaurus with a snowman?

Frostbite!

On which day do dinosaurs eat cavemen?

Chews-day!

What's big and scaly and goes round and round?

A stegosaurus on a turntable!

What does a T-Rex mum say to her kids at dinnertime?

Don't talk with cavemen in your mouth!

What time is it when a dinosaur sits on your garden wall?

Time to fix the wall!

How do you get five brontosaurus' into a Mini?

With difficulty!

What do you get if a diplodocus sits on your piano?

A flat note!

Why shouldn't
you dance
with a dinosaur?

Because if it trod on
you, you would get
flat feet!

What do you call a big, scary, disgruntled
T-Rex with cotton wool in its ears?

Anything you like, it can't hear you!

What happens if a dinosaur sits
in front of you at the cinema?

You miss most of the film!

A pair of T-Rex's are strolling around at
the seaside. One says to the other:

Funny, it's very quiet for a bank holiday!

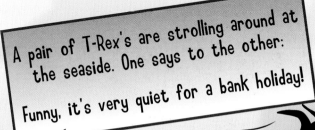

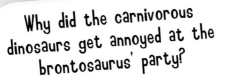

Why did the carnivorous dinosaurs get annoyed at the brontosaurus' party?

Because they only provided vegetarian food!

Where does Thomas the T-Rex sleep?

Anywhere he wants to!

Why did the diplodocus accidentally squash her boyfriend?

She had a crush on him!

What does a velociraptor eat in a restaurant?

The waiter!

What do young female T-Rex's do at parties?

They look for edible bachelors!

What is an archaeologist's favourite instrument?

A trom-bone!

How do archaeologists call their friends?

On the tele-bone!

Why did the skeletons enjoy the party in the Natural History Museum?

They had a rattling good time!

What do you call a fossil that won't get up in the morning?

Lazy bones!

What do you call a stupid dinosaur skeleton?

Bonehead!

How do dinosaurs greet each other?

Allo saurus!

How do you make a fossil laugh?

Tickle its funny bone!

What time is it when you see a velociraptor?

Time to run!

Where did the archaeopteryx meet her friend for coffee?

In the nest-café!

Where do the toughest dinosaurs come from?

Hard-boiled eggs!

Why did the dinosaur go to the orthodontist?

He wanted to improve his bite!

Where do prehistoric creatures go shopping?

The dino-store!

Why was the diplodocus wrinkly?

Have you even seen an iron big enough to straighten one out?!

What should you do if you find a dinosaur in your bed?

Sleep in the wardrobe!

What do prehistoric bank robbers use to blow open safes?

Dino-mite!

What do you get if a diplodocus sits down on your friend?

A flat mate!

What is the most common type of book in the prehistoric world?

A thesaurus!

What is the woolly mammoth's favourite mode of transport?

What do you get if you break a dinosaur egg?

A massive, massive omelette!

Why do velociraptors look forward to Christmas?

Because they will get a visit from Santa Claws!

Why did the T-Rex have the most painful mouth in the world?

He kept biting his tongue!

Who is safe when a man-eating dinosaur is on the rampage?

Women and children!

What do brontosaurus' use cavemen's bowling balls for?

To play marbles!

What was the cavemen's favourite fast food?

Kentucky fried brachiosaur!

Why is it useful to keep a triceratops in your house?

You can use it as a hat stand!

What is worse than a mammoth with a blocked up nose?

A brontosaurus with a stiff neck!

Knock knock!
Who's there?
Ivan.
Ivan who?
Ivan allosaurus and a T-Rex with me, so you'd better open up!

Why did
the archaeopteryx
go to the nightclub?

He wanted to meet
some chicks!

What do you get if you cross
a T-Rex with a boy scout?

A dinosaur that helps old
cavewomen across the road
and then eats them!

What do you call
an angry allosaurus?

Sir!

What's the time when a
mammoth gets in your bed?

Time to get a new bed!

Why was
the brachiosaurus
so forgetful?

He always had his head in
the clouds!

What is an ichthyothauruth?

An ichthyosaurus with a lisp!

What is the biggest and
warmest moth in the world?

A woolly mam-moth!

What is
the snobbiest dinosaur?

The pterodactyl, as it's a part
of 'high society'!

What do cavemen
eat with their tea?

Rock cakes!

Why did the two brontosaurus'
make the diplodocus blush?

Because they kept necking!

Who won the diplodocus race?

It was a draw. They finished neck and neck!

What is the favourite
fruit of the brachiosaur?

The neck-tarine!

What do cavemen have in common with Essex men?

They both wear leopard skin pants!

Why was the mammoth so good at playing the piano?

He liked to tinkle the ivories!

Where do triceratops go to build sandcastles?

At the Dino-shore!

What do you do when a mammoth is about to sneeze?

Run for cover!

How did
the mammoth find
his way home?

He followed his nose!

Where do mammoths
keep their valuables?

In their trunks!

What do yet get if you cross
a T-Rex with a watchdog?

A terrified postman!

Why was the diplodocus
so wrinkly?

It spent too long in the bath!

Book titles:

The Greediest Dinosaur
by Buster Gutt

Dinosaurs I have known
by O. Penjaw

Attack of the T-Rex
by Terry Fied

The Dinosaur Safety
Guide by Ron Fast

In the
Realm of the Dinosaurs
by Olive N. Fear

Dinosaur Dentistry
by Lara Bites

Sabre-Toothed Tiger
Recipes by Ethan Alive

Escape From
the Allosaurus
by Justin Time

The Cannibal Cavemen
by Ethan D. Lott

How to Provoke a Female
Dinosaur by Sheila Tack

The Velociraptor's Victim
by E. Drew Bludd

More book titles:

The Bad-Tempered Sabre-Tooth
by Claudia Armov

The Beginner's Guide to Dinosaur
Hunting by B. Warned

Chased by a Sabre-Tooth
by Claude Bottoms

Human Fossils
by Mandy Ceased

The Sabre-Tooth Book of
Nutrition by Nora Bone

Swimming With Ichthyosaurus
by Iris Keverything

How to Ride a Stegosaurus
by Major Bumsore

If you want to know more about sabre-toothed tigers, what do you do?

Join their fang club!

How do sabre-toothed tigers keep their houses smelling nice?

They use extractor fangs!

What do sabre-toothed tigers sing at the karaoke bar?

Fangs for the memories!

Why are sabre-toothed tigers so polite?

They always sang fangkyou!

What is a brontosaurus' most feared monster?

Vampires!

Why did the sabre-tooth give up acting?

He couldn't get his teeth into the part!

What did the sabre-tooth call his new false teeth?

A new fangled device!

Who did Miss Brontosaurus fancy?

The boy necks door!

What do an archaeopteryx and a taxman have in common?

Big bills!

Why do fossils learn Latin?

Because they like dead languages!

What is the most popular American football team among fossils?

The Washington Deadskins!

What did the skeleton's friend say when he was introduced to his new girlfriend?

Where did you dig her up from?!

Where do fossils go for their holidays?

The Deaditerranean!

How do you know a skeleton is tired?

He's dead on his feet!

What's huge and scaly and goes up and down?

A brontosaurus in a lift!

What do you get when a dinosaur does a sky dive?

A massive hole in the ground!

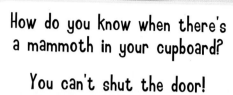

How do you know when there's a mammoth in your cupboard?

You can't shut the door!

What looks exactly like an iguanadon but weighs nothing?

An iguanadon's shadow!

What do you get if you cross a diplodocus with a kangaroo?

Big holes all over Australia!

What is the most popular holiday destination for mammoths?

Tusk-any!

What noise
do dinosaurs make in
their sleep?

Dino-snores!

What does the
T-Rex call his old girlfriend?

Tyrannosaurus ex!

Why was the archaeopteryx so big-headed?

He was popular with the chicks!

What do
cavemen say when they
split up with their girlfriends?

There's plenty more
ichthyosaurus' in
the sea!

What do you get if you attach wings onto a mammoth?

A jumbo jet!

What kind of beans do carnivorous dinosaurs like best?

Human beans!

Which dinosaur liked Mexican food?

Tyrannosaurus Mex!

What is big, scaly and scary and goes up and down?

A T-Rex on a trampoline!

What do you call a
hot-headed dinosaur?

Tyrannosaurus reckless!

How did
the mammoths react when
they found out the brontosaurus'
were being invaded?

They sent an international
tusk-force!

Why can't dinosaurs
swim in the sea?

Because tyrannosaurus wrecks!

Why did the allosaurus throw
up after he ate a vicar?

Because you can't keep a
good man down!

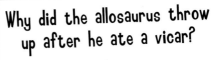

What do you call cautious, panicky dinosaurs?

Tyranno-nervous wrecks!

Who is the bossiest dinosaur?

Tyrant-saurus Rex!

Who is the laziest dinosaur?

Tired-saurus Rex!

What is the most popular science-fiction series in the prehistoric world?

Star T-Reks!

Who looks
after baby mammoths?

The woolly mum-moth!

What is the archaeopteryx's
favourite song?

I believe I can fly!

Who are the dinosaurs'
favourite soul band?

The Four Tricera-Tops!

Why did the caveman driver
get upset?

He got a Jurassic Parking ticket!

Why do lots of mammoths get sent to prison?

They get caught trunk-driving!

What do diplodocus' like to have for dessert?

Neckerbocker glories!

A mammoth walks into a bar. The barman says:

Why the long face?

A sabre-tooth walks into a bar. The barman says:

Why the big paws?

Why was the
ichthyosaurus suspicious?

He smelt something fishy!

What do you call a stupid
ichthyosaurus?

A thick-thyosaurus!

Why is a T-Rex like a computer?

Because it has mega-bites!

What do
you get if you cross
a sabre-toothed tiger
with a sausage?

A fang-furter!

What is the
dinosaurs' favourite film?

The Lizard of Oz.

What do
mammoths and owls have
in common?

They could both be described by
the phrase big hooters!

What do you get if you cross a
dinosaur with a cow and an oat field?

Mega lumpy porridge!

What did the ichthyosaurus
say to his long lost friend?

Long time no sea!

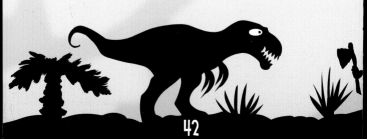

How do you know there's a dinosaur under your bed?

Your nose is pressed against the ceiling!

How do you find a lost diplodocus?

You'd have to be pretty stupid to lose one in the first place!

Why is it okay for a brontosaurus to wear a silly hat?

They're so tall no one can see them anyway!

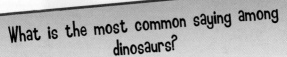

What is the most common saying among dinosaurs?

Red sky at night, dodge the meteorite.

Red sky in the morning, extinction warning!

Why are mammoths so woolly?

They'd look a bit stupid if they wore duffel coats!

How do you keep a smelly, ugly caveman in suspense?

I'll tell you tomorrow!

What dance do sabre-toothed tigers like best?

The fang-dango!

What do you call a sabre-toothed tiger who hates Australian soap operas?

A Neighbours-proof tiger!

What did the T-Rex say when he saw a group of sleeping cavemen?

Yum, breakfast in bed!

What do you call a dinosaur's underwear?

Tyrannosaurus' kecks!

What do dinosaurs use to mix records together?

Tyrannosaurus decks!

How did the dinosaur pay his bills?

With tyrannosaurus cheques!

What is archaeopteryx's favourite comedy series?

Birds of a Feather!

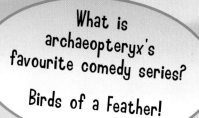

Why was the archaeopteryx treated with suspicion?

He was suspected of fowl play!

Why is an archaeopteryx so religious?

Because it is a bird of prey!

Why couldn't the mammoth go swimming?

He'd forgotten his trunks!

What was the
first ever ghost?

The terror-dactyl!

Which football
team do sabre-toothed
tigers support?

Fangchester United!

Who is an archaeopteryx's
favourite footballer?

David Peck'em!

Why did the archaeopteryx keep
getting sent off the football pitch?

He kept committing fowls!

What is
the sabre-toothed tiger's
favourite sixties song?

Wild fang!

How many cavemen does it take
to change a light bulb?

None, they weren't invented then!

Why did we run away from T-Rex?

Because the dinosaur us!

What do
you get if you cross a
mammoth with an ichthyosaur?

Swimming trunks!

What did the triceratops say when he was attacked by the T-Rex?

Nothing, triceratops can't talk!

Why are four-legged dinosaurs bad dancers?

Because they have two left feet!

What's 150 feet long and jumps every five seconds?

A diplodocus with the hiccups!

What do you call an ichthyosaur in the desert?

Lost!

What did Mr and
Mrs T-Rex call their baby?

Egg!

What was
Mr T-Rex's response when he
discovered his wife was pregnant?

Eggsellent!

What sport do
dinosaurs like best?

The egg and spoon race!

Why wasn't
the archaeopteryx invited
to dinner parties?

Because he used fowl language!

Which side of the triceratops
has the most scales?

The outside!

What did the archaeopteryx say
when she finished shopping?

Just put it on my bill!

What did the
dinosaur say when she
saw scrambled eggs?

Crazy mixed-up kid!

Why did the archaeopteryx
cross the football pitch?

He heard the referee calling fowls!

What do you give a sick dinosaur?

A very big paper bag!

What's big and scaly and very noisy?

A dinosaur with a drum kit!

Why do
dinosaurs live in
jungles and deserts?

Because they won't fit
in houses!

Why did the mammoth paint his feet yellow?

So he could hide upside down in custard!

Have you ever found a mammoth in custard?

No.

It must work then!

How many woolly mammoths does it take to make a jumper?

Woolly mammoths can't knit, idiot!

What would you do if a triceratops charged you?

Pay him cash!

Why is the sky so high?

So brachiosaurs won't bump their heads!

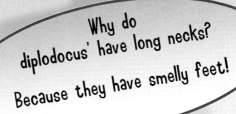

Why do
diplodocus' have long necks?

Because they have smelly feet!

What should you never do
when you meet a T-Rex?

Go to pieces!

What do you get if you
attack an archaeopteryx
with a lawn mower?

Shredded tweet!

Why do dinosaurs have big nostrils?

Because they have big fingers!

What did Mrs T-Rex say when she laid a square egg?

Ouch!

What's big and scaly and makes a horrible noise?

A dinosaur playing the bagpipes!

What is an archaeopteryx's favourite dish?

Anything that fits the bill!

What went into the sabre-toothed tiger's den and came out alive?

The sabre-toothed tiger!

What has four legs and can see just as well from both sides?

A brontosaurus with his eyes closed!

What do you get if you cross a sabre-toothed tiger with a lemon?

A sour puss!

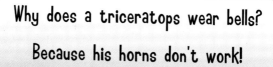

Why does a triceratops wear bells?

Because his horns don't work!

How do you stop a triceratops from charging?

Take away his credit card!

What do you do with a sick archaeopteryx?

Have it tweeted!

Why do dinosaurs eat raw meat?

Because they can't cook!

How does a dinosaur get down from a tree?

It sits on a leaf and waits for autumn!

Why did sabre-toothed tigers and woolly mammoths have unsightly teeth?

Because braces hadn't yet been invented!

Why did the
T-Rex spit out
the comedian?

Because he
tasted funny!

How do
you stop a
woolly mammoth
from smelling?

Tie its trunk into
a knot!

What is scaly, heavy and dark purple?

A diplodocus holding its breath!

Why did the triceratops run
over the caveman?

He forgot to sound his horns!

What do
you get if you
cross a porcupine and
a brontosaurus?

A massive
toothbrush!

What's big and scaly and hides in caves?

A velociraptor who owes money!

Why don't dinosaurs wear socks?

Because they'd look incredibly silly!

What do dinosaurs
put on their chips?

Tomatosaurus!

What do you call a dinosaur
who's been walking for six days?

My-feet-are-saurus!

Which dinosaur makes
the most noise when it sleeps?

Tyranno-snorus rex!

What do
you find at the rear end
of a triceratops?

His tricerabottom!

What has three horns, lots of
scales and sixteen wheels?

A triceratops on roller skates!

What's the
difference between a
dinosaur and a mouse?

A dinosaur is
CONSIDERABLY heavier!

What do you get if you
cross a pig with a diplodocus?

Gigantic pork chops!

What's worse than a
sabre-toothed tiger with toothache?

A brontosaurus with a sore throat!

Why do
brontosaurus' always get a
sore throat in winter?

Have you ever seen a scarf big enough
to keep their necks warm?

Which dinosaur grew rich when he discovered oil reserves?

Tyrannosaurus Tex!

What did the little volcano say to the big volcano?

Hi Cliff!

Small velociraptor: I hate this caveman's guts!

Large velociraptor: Just eat the rest then!

Why don't dinosaurs eat fish fingers?

Because human fingers taste much better!

Why did the
T-Rex get a medal?

He was a roaring success!

Who was the best dancer
at the dinosaur party?

Funk-asaurus!

What fur do you get from
a sabre-toothed tiger?

As fur away as possible!

What do
you call a stupid fossil?

Numbskull!

What do dinosaurs eat when they go to see the vet?

The vet!

Where do dinosaur skeletons go to play sport?

The golf corpse!

Why doesn't the T-Rex skeleton ever get annoyed?

Nothing gets under his skin!

Why are fossils always reluctant to wear shorts?

They have bony knees!

Why don't dinosaurs tell
their eggs jokes?

Because they'd crack up!

What do you call a dinosaur
who rides horses in a rodeo?

Bronco-saurus!

What do
you do if you're
chased by a
co-operative triceratops?

Make a reverse-
charge call!

What cereal do triceratops'
eat for breakfast?

Horn flakes!

What is a triceratops'
favourite instrument?

The French horn!

What is
a triceratops'
favourite TV programme?

Hornblower!

Where do you find most brontosaurus'?

Between their heads and tails!

Why was the diplodocus so wrinkly?

He was always worried!

What do you call a sweet, pleasant, non-aggressive T-Rex?

A resounding failure!

What do you get if you cross a diplodocus with a mallard?

Diplo-duck-us!

Do brontosaurus' catch head colds if they get their feet wet?

Yes, but it takes a fortnight to reach that far!

What do dinosaurs and coins have in common?

They both have a head and tail!

What do dinosaurs and coins not have in common?

You can't toss a dinosaur!

Who are the snootiest dinosaurs?

Diplodocus', because they look down on everyone!

Why did the caveman fall in love with the T-Rex?

It was love at first fright!

What do skeletons say when they are annoyed?

I've got a bone to pick with you!

What did the T-Rex say when he saw Seven Brides for Seven Brothers?

Mmm, lunch!

What is one of the dinosaurs' favourite sitcoms?

Allo allo-saurus!

Who is the dirtiest, smelliest dinosaur?

Steg(osaurus) of the dump!

Why did the plesiosaur visit Scotland?

To find his long lost cousin Nessie!

What is the dinosaur's favourite hair care product?

Allo-vera-saurus!

What do dinosaur police say?

'Allo 'allo 'allosaurus!

Where does the vegetarian allosaurus grow his turnips?

In his Allo-tment!

What do you call a T-Rex working as an office messenger?

Tyrannosaurus Fax!

What do you call a dinosaur who is a jazz musician?

Tyrannosaurus Sax!

What do you call a particularly bendy dinosaur?

Tyrannosaurus Flex!

What do you call a dinosaur who comes from the middle east?

Iran-osaurus Rex!

What do you get if you cross a diplodocus with a T-Rex?

Tyrannosaurus Necks!

What do you get if you cross a diplodocus with a children's toy?

Duplo-docus!

What do you get if you cross a dinosaur with a children's toy?

Lego-saurus!

Why was the stegosaurus such a good waiter?

He was used to carrying lots of plates!

Why was the stegosaurus scared to go in a Greek restaurant?

He was worried they'd smash his plates!

Where do mammoths go on holiday?

The Ivory Coast!

Why don't mammoths eat eggs?

Because they are scared of poachers!

Why did the baby dinosaur get over-excited?

The others kept egging him on!

Why did the baby dinosaur think his newborn sister was mad?

She was cracking up!

What are baby dinosaurs' favourite vegetables?

Eggplants!

Why did everyone think the mammoth was really old?

He was long in the tooth!

What London tube station do mammoths like to travel to?

Toothing Broadway!

Why was the sabre-toothed tiger very lucky to escape the T-Rex?

He escaped by the skin of his teeth!

What do dinosaurs
have for dessert?

Diplodocustard!

What do you call a dinosaur from Ireland?

Bront O'Saurus!

Did you hear about the
prehistoric magician?

He dino-sawed his assistant in half!

What do you call a dinosaur
who has accidentally bitten
his tongue?

Tyrannothauruth reckth!

How do you stop a
brontosaurus from coughing?

Tie his neck in a knot!

Why was the mammoth late to the airport?

He had difficulty packing his trunk.

What do you call a
diplodocus with vertigo?

Very, very unlucky!

What nickname did they give the
wrinkly, rough skinned dinosaur?

Prunella Scales!

Where do archaeologists usually find fossilised sabre-toothed tigers?

In cat-acombs!

Why was it so sad when the sabre-tooth tigers died out?

It was a cat-astrophe!

Where do sabre-toothed tigers take their post?

To the cat-a-pillar box!

Why did Mr and Mrs Sabre Tooth get divorced?

They'd lost that lovin' feline!

Why did the sabre tooth
leave school early?

He was feline ill!

Why don't you ever get sabre-toothed
tigers refereeing football matches?

Because they are make much
better Fe-linesmen!

What tangy sweet
do dinosaurs like best?

Sherbet diplodocus!

What did the diplodocus say
on his way to the swimming pool?

Just off for a quick dip!

What do you call a
really stupid
dinosaur?

Dippy-lodocus!

What is the skeletons' favourite
Kylie Minogue song?

'I Can't Get You Out of My Skull'!

What is the most famous
group of singing dinosaurs?

The Bronto-chorus!

What's like a plague of
locusts but much heavier?

A plague of diplodocusts!

What did the dinosaur call his auntie and uncle's children?

His diplodo-cousins!

Why did everyone like the baby dinosaur?

They thought he was a good egg!

Why did cavemen smell so bad?

Soap hadn't been invented!

What is the most popular prehistoric toy shop?

Dinosau-R-Us!

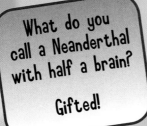

What do you call a Neanderthal with half a brain?

Gifted!

What is the Neanderthals' favourite Mel Gibson film?

Cave-heart!

Why did the Neanderthals die out?

Their caves were too smelly to die in!

What is the Neanderthals' favourite themed restaurant?

The 50s diner-saur!

Why don't you get
Neanderthal omelette
restaurants anymore?

Because they are eggs-tinct!

Why did the T-Rex keep a box of six-foot
wooden fence posts at his dinner table?

In case he needed any toothpicks!

Why did the Neanderthal man
keep losing his money?

The wallet hadn't yet been invented!

What is the dinosaurs'
favourite Kylie Minogue song?

'The Diplodocomotion'!

Where do dinosaurs
go when they feel ill?

The Diplo-doctor!

What is the Neanderthals'
favourite home improvement show?

Changing Caves!

What weapon
did the caveman only
carry after it got dark?

His night-club!

Why did the Neanderthal have to
go to the dentist to get fillings?

He had tooth cave-ities!

What do you call a sabre-toothed tiger that has watched too much science fiction?

A light sabre-toothed tiger!

Why couldn't the caveman ring the doorbell when he visited his friend?

The doorbell hadn't yet been invented!

Why didn't he knock on the door then?

The door hadn't been invented either!

Why was the Neanderthal so proud of his damp, smelly, rocky hole?

Because a Neanderthal Man's cave is his castle!

What do cavemen use to fix things?

Neander-tools!

What is the definition of disgust?

A Neanderthal picking his nose and eating it, while sitting in a prehistoric compost heap! YUCK!

Why do Neanderthals eat with their mouths open?

Flies have got to live somewhere!

In the prehistoric world, the dinosaurs believe one 'right' is always 'wrong'. Which 'right' is it?

The meteor-right!

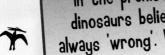

What did they call the seven-foot caveman?

Neander-tall!

What is a worse place to be than a frequently used cesspit?

A Neanderthal's armpit!

Why do Neanderthals' have such hairy faces?

So they don't have to wear paper bags over their heads!

Why did the Neanderthal win the beauty contest?

All the other contestants suddenly became extinct!

How do
you get a one-armed
Neanderthal out of a tree?

Wave at him!

What do you do if a Neanderthal
throws a hand grenade at you?

Take out the pin and throw it back!

How do you confuse a Neanderthal?

Put him in a round room and
tell him to sit in the corner!

Why did
the Neanderthal get sacked
from the banana factory?

He kept throwing out the
bent ones!

What do you get if you cross a diplodocus with a big box of laxatives?

As far away as possible!

What is the soft stuff between ichthyosaur teeth?

Slow swimmers!

What is the soft, thick stuff between T-Rex teeth?

Slow Neanderthals!

What did the dinosaurs warn their guests when a triceratops got in a bowl of fruit and wine at the party?

Be careful, someone spiked the punch!

Why are triceratops' not allowed to be cowboys?

They make holes in the ten-gallon hats!

What is the dinosaurs' favourite music programme?

Top of the Tricera-pops!

What do dinosaurs put on their pizzas?

Tricera-topping!

What was the cave-baby's favourite toy?

His spinning tricera-top!

Which cartoon characters advertised prehistoric breakfast cereal?

Snap, Crackle and Tricera-Pops!

What do smart dinosaurs wear to dinner parties?

A shirt and Tie-rannosaurus Rex!

What did they call the over-emotional dinosaur?

Cry-annosaurus Rex!

What do cavemen blow their noses on?

Tyrannosaurus Cleenex!

Where do religious dinosaurs go to buy snacks?

The friar tuck-shop!

What did the dinosaurs call the wimpy ichthyosaur?

The sea-weed!

Why did the diplodocus fail the interview to be a TV presenter?

They couldn't fit his neck into the screen!

Who was the prehistoric policeman?

PC Plod-ocus!

What do
you call a
super-intelligent dinosaur?

An Oxford iguana-don!

What do Greek Neanderthals eat?

Iguana-doner kebabs!

Where do cavemen go to
get braces put on their teeth?

The iguana-dontist!

What do you call a dinosaur with
an extremely large appetite?

Pig-uanadon!

What do dinosaurs use to drill for oil?

An oil rig-uanadon!

What do Neanderthals do when they go to a football match and their team scores a goal?

A Mexican Cave!

What do you call an annoying dinosaur?

Iguanadon't care!

What do you call a prehistoric cat that sits on top of a cave swearing at passers-by?

An uncouth sabre-tooth on a roof!

Why did the Neanderthal put a solid steel door on his cave?

Because it was sabre tooth proof!

Why do sabre-toothed tigers buy their clothes through the post?

They like to use cat-alogues!

What do you call a Neanderthal with no sense of smell?

Very lucky!

Why didn't Neanderthals use deodorant?

It hadn't been invented yet!

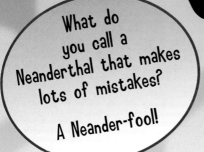

What do
you call a
Neanderthal that makes
lots of mistakes?

A Neander-fool!

Who is the dinosaurs'
favourite film character?

Ichthy-ana Jones!

Who is the most exciting
skeleton in the museum?

Indiana Bones!

Which dish was most popular in
the skeleton restaurant?

Spare ribs!

Why was
the skeleton
always so lonely?

Because he had nobody!

What do you get if you
cross a T-Rex and a parrot?

I don't know, but when it
talks you'd better listen!

How did the Neanderthal call his mum?

On a smellular phone!

Why didn't the Neanderthal witch
cast any spells?

She was too busy casting smells!

What do you
do if you catch a
group of Neanderthals
eating baked beans?

Get as far away
as possible!

Why didn't Neanderthals use clothes
pegs on their washing lines?

They used them all up on their noses!

Why did the Neanderthal
climb over the glass wall?

He wanted to see what
was on the other side!

What does
a diplodocus do if
she breaks her toe?

She calls a toe-truck!

Why did mammoths have big trunks?

They hadn't invented the rucksack yet!

How do you stop a Neanderthal from smelling?

Put corks in his nose!

What do you get if you knit with Neanderthal hair?

Foul-smelling jumpers!

What pets do every single Neanderthal have, whether they want them or not?

Fleas, ticks, tapeworms and flies!

What do French cheese and Neanderthals have in common?

They both smell awful!

What did one flea say to the other after a night out?

Shall we walk home or take the dinosaur?

Where do dinosaurs go if they think they need glasses?

The archae-optician!

Which action/adventure film do dinosaurs like best?

Raiders of the Lost Archaeopteryx!

Which science-fiction films do Neanderthals like best?

Star Warts!

What is one of the dinosaurs' favourite comedy series?

Goodness Cretaceous Me!

Which Victorian book do dinosaurs like best?

Archaeoliver Twist!

Why didn't cavemen like 'Knock Knock' jokes?

Because the door hadn't yet been invented!

What do you call a theme park full of prehistoric dogs?

Jurassic Bark!

What do vegetarian dinosaurs fear even more than meteorites?

Meat-eorites!

What do you call a dinosaur hunter?

Very, very brave!

What is the Neanderthals' favourite western film?

The Ugly, the Smelly and the Even Uglier!

What did
the dinosaur
say to his new
caveman friend?

I'd like to get to
gnaw you.

What did he say ten minutes later?

It's been nice gnawing you!

What do you call a dinosaur that
has lots of tedious stories about the sea?

An ichthyo-bore-us!

What do
you call a dinosaur that gets
things done extremely quickly?

Pronto-saurus!

What do you call
a dinosaur that makes
lots of smart-alec jokes?

Sarky-opteryx!

Why did the mammoth spend
the night in a police cell?

He was trunk and disorderly!

Why do you call a sabre tooth
who specialises in robbery?

A cat burglar!

How often do Neanderthals have a bath?

Once a year, whether they need it or not!

What do you get if you cross an archaeopteryx with a sabre-toothed tiger?

A cat flap!

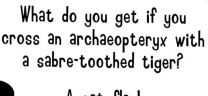

What do you get if a dinosaur sits on your top hat?

A flat cap!

What do you call a triceratops with blunt horns?

A failure!

What do you call an ichthyosaur who can't swim?

A failure!

What do you get if you cross an ichthyosaur with an archaeopteryx?

Water wings!

What do you do if you hear a dinosaur with a rumbling stomach?

Run away!

Why is it very easy being a prehistoric policeman?

Dinosaur fingerprints aren't difficult to find!

What does a T-Rex call a group of cavemen covered in custard?

Dessert!

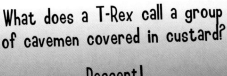

What do
you need to keep a pet
ichthyosaur?

A very large tank!

Why did the mammoths blush?

Their trunks fell down!

What do mammoths do if they get
close to a group of Neanderthals?

Tie their trunks in a knot!

What do you get if you put
a T-Rex in your freezer?

Frostbite!

Which shop do skeletons like best?

The Body shop!

Why did everyone think the pterodactyl was vain?

He kept looking in his wing-mirrors!

Why don't cavemen keep sabre-toothed tigers as pets?

Imagine what the litter tray would be like!

What do waiters say if you ask for a plate of brontosaurus in a restaurant?

That's a tall order!

What did the vampire say the first time he saw a diplodocus?

I just don't know where to start!

Knock knock!
Who's there?
Doughnut.
Doughnut who?
Doughnut go near a hungry T-Rex!

Knock knock!
Who's there?
Clara.
Clara who?
Clara path! The brontosaurus stampede is coming this way!

Knock knock!
Who's there?
Wendy.
Wendy who?
Wendy T-Rex heads this way, run like hell!

What do you get if you cross a Neanderthal with a diplodocus?

The world's biggest stinker!

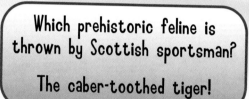

Which prehistoric feline is thrown by Scottish sportsman?

The caber-toothed tiger!

What do woolly mammoths use to play catch?

A fur ball!

What do you call a sissy woolly mammoth?

A frilly mammoth!

Which dinosaurs can fly?

Ones with airline tickets!

Why did the skeleton confuse his doctor?

He claimed to be having an out-of-body experience!

What's scarier than a gang of hungry tyrannosaurs?

A gang of hungry tyrannosaurs with machine guns!

What did the T-Rex, the allosaurus, the sabre-toothed tiger and the velociraptor call their gang?

The fearsome foursome!

What did the sabre-toothed tiger and the woolly mammoth call their gang?

The toothsome twosome!

What did everyone say whenever the woolly mammoth came up with an idea?

Another hair-brained scheme!

What did everyone say to the triceratops who talked too much?

Get to the point!

What did the barman say to the triceratops who came into his pub?

Will that be three points then, sir?

What do you get if you cross dinosaurs with sabre-toothed tigers?

Dino-paws!

Why did the T-Rex keep a light bulb in his mouth?

He wanted a nice bright smile!

Why was the T-Rex always short of cash?

He had to spend a fortune on toothpaste!

Why did everyone think the skeleton was mad?

He had decided to become a body builder!

Why were the dinosaurs good at exams?

They always passed with extinction!

Why did everyone think the skeleton was a coward?

He had no guts!

Why did the sabre-toothed tiger hate small rooms?

He suffered from claws-trophobia!

What stories do woolly mammoths tell their children?

Furry tales!

Knock knock!
Who's there?
Ewell.
Ewell who?
Ewell be sorry if you upset a velociraptor!

What do dinosaurs use when they do their farming?

A veloci-tractor!

Which dinosaur is the biggest hip-hop fan?

The veloci-rapper!

What did the man-eating dinosaur say when he was offered some shepherd's pie?

Is it made of real shepherds?

Why was the caveman pleased to hear the Ice Age was coming?

He needed to chill out!

What do you call an aggressive woolly mammoth?

A bully mammoth!

What do you call a stupid woolly mammoth?

A wally mammoth!

Why did the extinct dinosaur write music that went backwards?

He was de-composing!

Why did the decomposing dinosaur stay in bed all day?

Because he felt rotten!

What do skeletons use to make their crockery?

Bone china!

What is the most famous painting of a skeleton?

The Bona Lisa!

What competition do skeleton parents enter their children in?

The boney baby contest!

Which rock band do
skeletons like best?

Bone Jovi!

What do
skeletons say before they eat?

Bone appetite!

What do
French dinosaurs say instead of hello?

Bone jour!

Why was the skeleton tired after work?

He'd worked his fingers to the bone!

How do you make a
skeleton laugh?

Tell him a rib-tickling joke!

What did Mr and Mrs Skeleton
name their twin daughters?

Fibula and Tibia!

Why did the skeleton enjoy
the roller coaster?

It was a bare-knuckle ride!

Which Shakespeare
play do skeletons like best?

Boneo and Juliet!

Why did the woolly mammoth always annoy the other dinosaurs?

He was always sticking his nose in other people's business!

Which mammoth could see into the future?

Nose-stradamus!

Why do brontosaurus' have such long necks?

Because they like to wear lots of medallions!

Which Central American country do diplodocus' like to go to on holiday?

Neckaragua!

How do you cut a
pterodactyl in half?

With a dinosaw.

Why couldn't
the skeleton ring home to say
he was going to be late for dinner?

He had forgotten to charge his
mobile bone!

Why did the dinosaur go hungry?

Because T-Rex.

Which TV comedy do
skeletons like best?

One Foot in the Grave!

What do skeletons use to keep their hair nice and neat?

A cata-comb!

Why can't you make a dinosaur sandwich?

Because you can't get bread big enough!

Why did the T-Rex have an upset stomach?

Because she ate someone who disagreed with her!

Where do you find sabre-toothed tigers modelling new clothes?

On the catwalk!

What's the difference between a dinosaur and a biscuit?

You can't dunk a dinosaur in your tea!

What do you call a dinosaur's practical joke?

A Jurassic lark!

What came first, the dinosaur or the egg?

I'm afraid I have no eggs-planation for that riddle!

What do you do if a dinosaur comes to your picnic?

Give it the hamper and run like mad!

What do dinosaurs use to make beer?

Tricera-hops!

A man walks into a restaurant and asks the waiter:
"Do you serve Scotsmen?"
"Certainly, sir," says the waiter.
"Good. I'll have a steak and two Scotsmen for my pet dinosaur."

A boy walks into a museum, and sees a big dinosaur skeleton. He asks the museum attendant:
"How old is that skeleton?"
"Three million and eleven years," replies, the attendant.
"How do you know about the eleven years?" says the boy.
"Well," he says, "I started work here eleven years ago, and it was three million years old then!"

What do you sit a baby diplodocus on?

A high chair!

In the Arctic, where do baby dinosaurs live?

In egg-loos!

Why do sabre-toothed tigers admire Robin Hood?

Because he robbed from the rich, and gave to the paw!

Why did the baby diplodocus think it was hailing?

His mum had terrible dandruff!

Why did the T-Rex have athlete's foot?

He'd already eaten the rest of the athlete and felt a bit full!

Why do diplodocus' wear hats with flashing red lights on them?

So planes don't crash into their heads!

Why did Mr Brontosaurus build a giant garden fence?

Mr Diplodocus, his neighbour, was very nosy!

What do you call a woolly mammoth who drives a car for Lady Penelope?

Nosy Parker!

What is worse than a T-Rex with bad breath?

A mammoth with bad nasal hair!

Why did
the T-Rex have a
sore throat?

It was red roar!

Why don't dinosaurs wear shoes?

Have you ever seen a shoe big
enough for a dinosaur?!

What do you get if you cross
a mammoth with a kangaroo?

A woolly jumper!

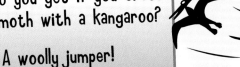

Who is the most popular
dinosaur astrologer?

Bronto-taurus!

Why was the herd of diplodocus
seen as a group of liars?

They had lots of tall tails!

What do you get if you cross
a T-Rex and a snail?

A very slow carnivore in a crash helmet!

What flowers do
tyrannosaurs like best?

Snapdragons!

Why did the caveman go from the
triceratops tail to its head?

His friends told him to get to the point!

What's more dangerous than kissing a T-Rex?

Head butting a triceratops!

Why did everyone think the iguanadon was pleased with everything?

He was always giving them a thumbs-up!

Neanderthal: I've just come back from the beauty parlour.

Caveman: Pity it was closed!

Why did everyone think the geriatric archaeopteryx was a policeman?

Because everyone called him 'the Old Bill'!

What do dinosaurs put in their sausages?

Jurassic pork!

What snack do dinosaurs eat when they go to the pub?

Jurassic pork scratchings!

Why did the triceratops blush?

Because the bronto-swore-at-us!

Why don't you see dinosaurs at the zoo?

They prefer to go to the cinema!

What do you call a Neanderthal who once put his right arm in a T-Rex's mouth?

Lefty!

What do get if you cross a brontosaurus with a rooster?

An alarm clock for people who live in tall buildings!

Young Neanderthal: Everyone says I'm ugly.

Mrs Neanderthal: Nonsense son. Now comb your face and go out to play!

What's the difference between a diplodocus and a letter?

Have you ever tried fitting a diplodocus into a postbox?!

What do tables and stegosaurus' have in common?

They have four legs and keep plates on their back!

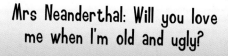

Mrs Neanderthal: Will you love me when I'm old and ugly?

Mr Neanderthal: Of course I do!

Why was the triceratops such a successful boxer?

He always won on points!

Why was the triceratops bad at telling other dinosaurs directions?

He was always pointing in three directions at once!

What did the T-Rex say to the argumentative triceratops?

I can see your point.

Why don't you get triceratops' with flat heads?
Because that would be pointless!

Why did the mammoths have an argument at the swimming pool?

Because they only had one pair of trunks between them!

What happened to Ray the caveman when he was attacked by a T-Rex?

He became an X-ray!

What do you call a caveman who keeps well away from dinosaurs?

Sensible!

Why did prehistoric woolly hats often have three holes?

So triceratops' could keep their heads warm!

Which dinosaur always refuses to give up?

A try-try-try-ceratops!

Why wouldn't the dinosaurs let the velociraptors join in their game of football?

Because their claws always burst the ball!

What is
the difference
between a T-Rex and a
gentle dog?

A T-Rex's bite is much,
much, much worse
than his bark!

What kind of baby would
thrive on diplodocus milk?

A baby diplodocus!

What should you cook if a T-Rex
comes to your house for dinner?

Your family!

What is the
most common name
for a triceratops?

Spike!

What is the second most
common name for a triceratops?

Lance!

What do dinosaurs use
instead of a dictionary?

A dinothesaurus!

Why do museums only have old
bones in them?

They can't afford to buy any new ones!

Was the
Neanderthal model
pretty or ugly?

Both, she was
pretty ugly!

What is
the velociraptors'
favourite card game?

Snap!

Why did the brontosaurus
consume an entire car factory?

Because he was a plant eater!

What do you call an archaeopteryx
attached to a plug and socket?

An electricity bill!

What do you call an archaeopteryx
who never shuts up?

A gas bill!

Why did the archaeopteryx never play snooker?

He preferred bill-iards!

What do you call a diplodocus pirate?

Long Neck Silver!

What do you get if you cross a box of medical equipment with a new-born sabre tooth cub?

A first-aid kitty!

What's worse than being hit by pigeon droppings?

Being hit by archaeopteryx droppings!

Mr T-Rex:
I've brought a
friend home for dinner.

Mrs T-Rex: How would
you like him? Boiled
or fried?

Why was the brontosaurus
the poorest dinosaur?

Because he owned necks
to nothing!

What's big, scary, scaly and red all over?

An embarrassed dinosaur!

Where do Mr and Mrs Mammoth
keep their children?

In the cub-board!

When do young sabre-toothed tigers wear caps and scarves?

When they join the cubs!

Why was the mammoth turned away from the airport?

They said his trunks wouldn't fit on the plane!

Mrs Caveman: I'm a bit skinny. Could you suggest a good way of putting on weight?

Dr Caveman: Try carrying a brontosaurus on your shoulders!

Why do Neanderthals always get up really late?

They need an awful lot of beauty sleep!

A dinosaur goes into a café and asks
for a fizzy drink.
"That'll be three pounds," says the waiter.
As the dinosaur drinks, the barman says
"We don't get many dinosaurs in here."
"I'm not surprised at three pounds a drink,"
says the dinosaur.

What is
ichthyosaurus' favourite curry?

Fin-daloo!

Why did the
T-Rex wear dark
glasses on holiday?

He was trying not
to be noticed!

Here's a good joke,
two dinosaurs fell
off a cliff.
BOOM BOOM!

Why do
mammoths go
to peaceful places
for their holidays?

They enjoy
trunkwility!

What did the T-Rex say when he
saw a group of cavemen riding
around on their motorbikes?

Ah, meals on wheels!

Why was the triceratops always
so well dressed?

He always looked sharp!

What do iguanadons
do when they're bored?

Twiddle their thumbs!

Which children's story
do iguanadons like best?

Tom Thumb!

What happened
to Batman and Robin when a
diplodocus sat on them?

They changed their names to
Flatman and Ribbon!

What's the best way to raise a
baby diplodocus?

A gigantic crane usually does the trick!

What do practical jokers do to
mammoths instead of tying their shoelaces?

Tie their trunks!

What do you do if a mammoth faints?

Give it trunk-to-trunk resuscitation!

What do you do if a dinosaur won't fit in the back of your car?

Let it sit in the front!

Which dinosaurs can be found on a chessboard?

Tyrannosaurus Rooks!

Why don't mammoths join the army?

Because they're better suited to the hair force!

Why were there
lots of earthquakes in
the prehistoric era?

Because the diplodocus
kept getting hiccups!

What's the difference between a hungry
velociraptor and a greedy T-Rex?

One longs to eat, the other eats too long!

At what time of day did the T-Rex
eat the prime minister?

Ate PM!

How long are brontosaurus' legs?

Long enough to reach the ground!